THE REVOLUTIONARY WAR

HOW AMERICA WON ITS INDEPENDENCE

JOHN MALAM

SCHOLASTIC
www.scholastic.com

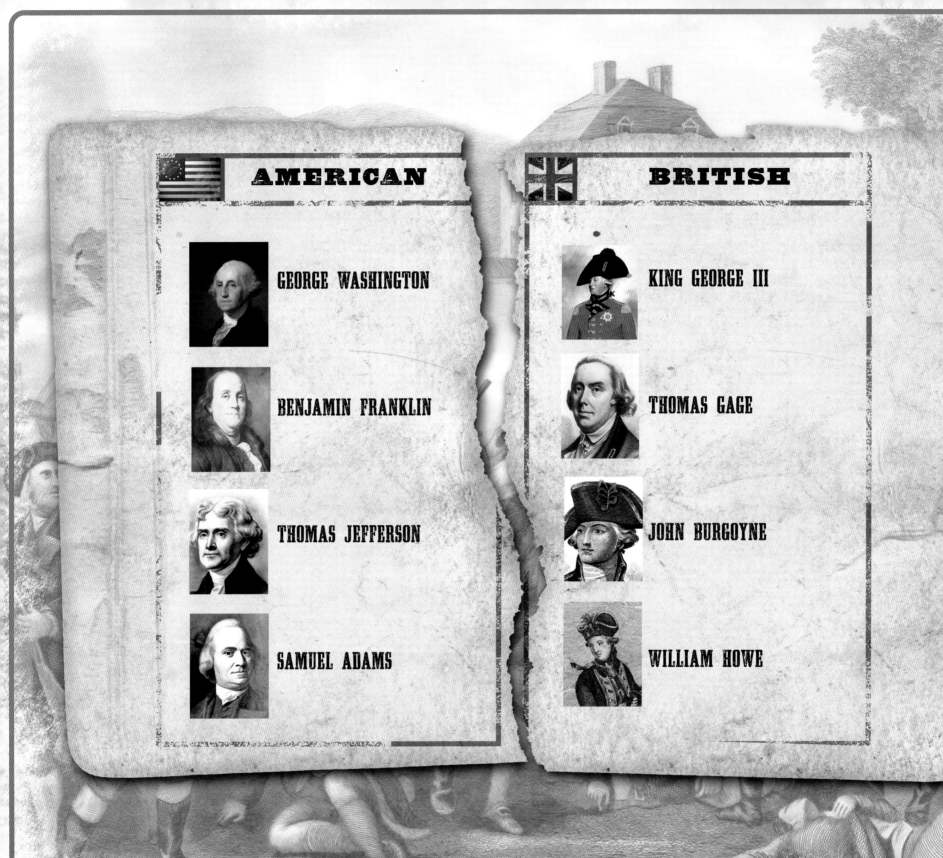

AMERICAN

GEORGE WASHINGTON

BENJAMIN FRANKLIN

THOMAS JEFFERSON

SAMUEL ADAMS

BRITISH

KING GEORGE III

THOMAS GAGE

JOHN BURGOYNE

WILLIAM HOWE

INTRODUCTION

The Revolutionary War of 1775–1783 gave birth to a nation.

By the middle of the 1700s, Britain's colonies on the East Coast of North America were well established, with over a hundred years of history behind them. Although Britain was thousands of miles away across the sea, connections with the mother country were still strong.

Most people thought of themselves as belonging to a particular colony, as being Virginians or New Yorkers, rather than Americans. Yet in the course of the Revolutionary War, the thirteen colonies were transformed into states in a newborn nation. That nation would go on to become the greatest superpower the world has ever known.

Why did the colonies break away from Britain, and how did they do it? This book looks at the eight-year conflict that created the United States.

THIRTEEN COLONIES

In 1763, a group of men from Britain, France, and Spain met in Paris, the capital city of France.

Their countries had been at war with each other over who was the world's superpower, but now they came together to sign a peace treaty. Known as the Treaty of Paris, it brought the Seven Years' War to an end. More than 30 battles had been fought in Europe, Africa, India, and the West Indies, but nowhere were the consequences as great as in North America.

A map from the 1700s showing the Americas.

THE WAR IN NORTH AMERICA

In North America, the Seven Years' War was known as the French and Indian War. It began in 1754 and was mainly fought between Britain and France, both of whom had colonies there. Each country wanted to be the controlling power in North America.

This modern map shows the 3,500 miles of ocean that separate America and Britain.

A BRITISH VICTORY

At first, all went well for France. Then, in 1757, Britain fought back by sending an extra 25,000 troops. As well as these new British soldiers, Britain raised an army of 25,000 American soldiers. This was a militia army—a military force of civilians whose job was to support the regular British army. The men came from Britain's North American territories—a group of thirteen **colonies** located along the Atlantic coast. By 1760 Britain had won the war in North America.

PEACE BEFORE THE STORM

By 1763, most people who lived in Britain's American colonies had been born there, and few had visited the "mother country." Britain's North American colonies were ruled by Britain from Britain. To put it another way, two million American people were not in control of their own lives.

The **peace treaty** that Britain made with her old enemy France may have ended one war, but it sowed the seeds for a new war and the birth of a new nation—the United States of America.

GEOR

MAINE
(part of
Massachusetts)

NEW HAMPSHIRE

NEW YORK

MASSACHUSETTS

RHODE ISLAND

CONNECTICUT

PENNSYLVANIA

NEW JERSEY

DELAWARE
(part of Pennsylvania)

MARYLAND

VIRGINIA

NORTH
CAROLINA

THE COLONIES

Britain's colonies in North America are often referred to as the First British Empire. They were prosperous territories with growing populations. By the 1760s there were many large towns and thousands of farms.

Colony	Date founded
Virginia	1607
Massachusetts	1620
New Hampshire	1623
Connecticut	1633
Maryland	1634
Rhode Island	1636
Delaware	1638
North Carolina	1663
New Jersey	1664
New York	1664
South Carolina	1670
Pennsylvania	1681
Georgia	1733

❧ WINNERS AND LOSERS ☙

★ ★ ★ ★ ★ ★ ★ ★

The Treaty of Paris gave Britain control over almost the whole of North America. Under the terms of the treaty:

☆ Britain took control of Canada and all French territory east of the Mississippi River;
☆ Britain took control of Florida from Spain;
☆ Spain took control of Louisiana from France.

KING GEORGE III

The people of Britain's American colonies were expected to be loyal to the British king, George III. He became king in 1760, and although he never visited his American territories, his government officials kept him up to date with news. However, within a few years of the Treaty of Paris being signed, history was to record King George III as "the king who lost America."

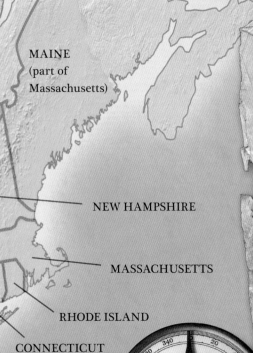

TAXING THE COLONIES

When the French and Indian War ended, the British government was left with a big problem—how to pay for it.

By 1763, Britain had borrowed about £137 million. But the country was only earning about £8 million per year. Britain had to find a way of paying its debts.

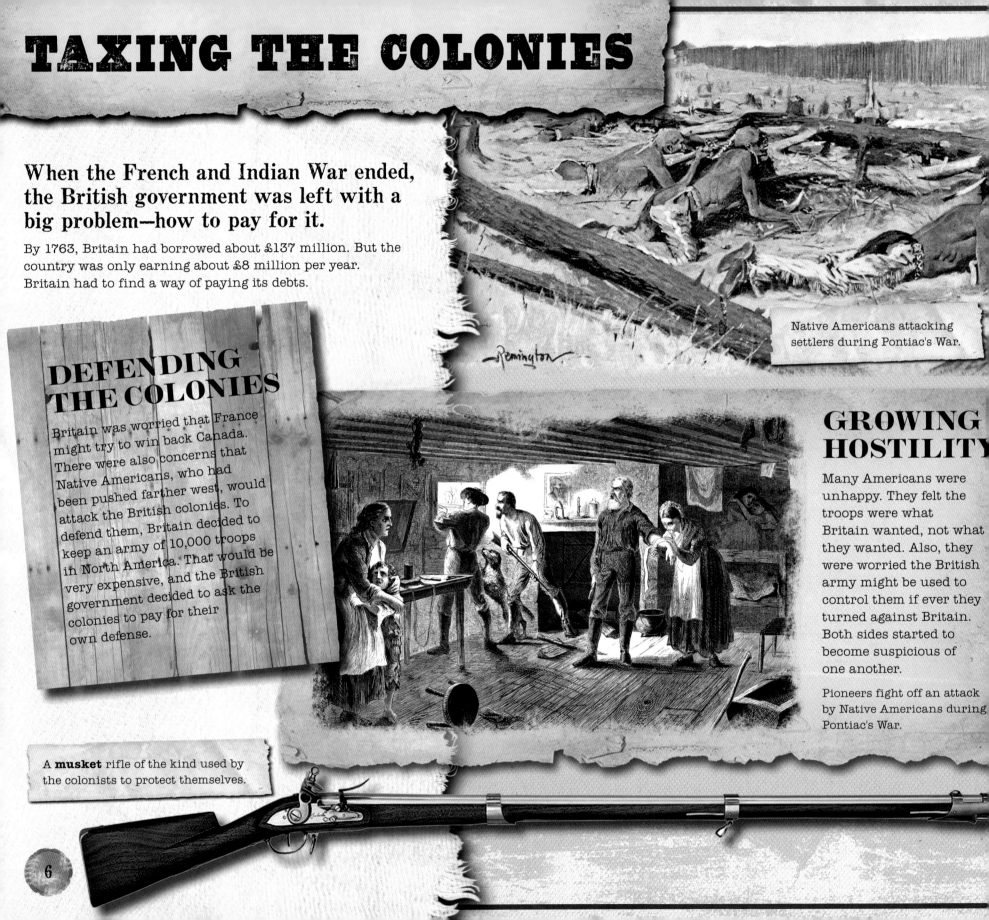

Native Americans attacking settlers during Pontiac's War.

DEFENDING THE COLONIES

Britain was worried that France might try to win back Canada. There were also concerns that Native Americans, who had been pushed farther west, would attack the British colonies. To defend them, Britain decided to keep an army of 10,000 troops in North America. That would be very expensive, and the British government decided to ask the colonies to pay for their own defense.

GROWING HOSTILITY

Many Americans were unhappy. They felt the troops were what Britain wanted, not what they wanted. Also, they were worried the British army might be used to control them if ever they turned against Britain. Both sides started to become suspicious of one another.

Pioneers fight off an attack by Native Americans during Pontiac's War.

A **musket** rifle of the kind used by the colonists to protect themselves.

NATIVE AMERICAN ATTACK

Trouble did come, from Native Americans who feared losing more of their land to settlers moving west from the British colonies. In 1763, tribes attacked and destroyed British forts in the Great Lakes region. Hundreds of settlers were killed or captured. One of the tribes most involved was the Ottawa people. Their leader was Pontiac, and the uprising bears his name—Pontiac's War, or Pontiac's **Rebellion**.

UNEASY TRUCE

The British army fought back and the uprising was soon over, though neither side could claim outright victory. Britain decided to draw a boundary line along part of the Appalachian mountain range. Native American lands were to the west of the line; British colonies were to the east.

The idea was to calm the fears of Native Americans by putting their homelands out of bounds to white settlers. But many Americans in the colonies opposed the boundary. They thought that Britain supported the Native Americans, and they ignored the British plan. By 1768, up to 30,000 white settlers are believed to have crossed the boundary onto land set aside for Native Americans.

A British soldier from the 48th Foot Regiment.

SMUGGLING

For many years, American merchants had been **smuggling** sugar and molasses into the colonies as a way of avoiding paying taxes to Britain.

The British government tried to stop smuggling by lowering the amount of tax on these goods. It was a simple idea. If there was less tax to pay, merchants would pay it to avoid being fined if caught. For Britain, it seemed like a win-win plan—taxes would be paid and smuggling would stop.

THE STAMP ACT

Britain's next move was to make people in the colonies pay a new tax. For this to happen, a law had to be passed in Britain. The law, called the Stamp Act, put a tax on about 50 different kinds of paper items printed in the colonies. Even school diplomas were to be taxed. To show the tax had been paid, the paper items would be marked with a special tax stamp.

The real stamp looked like this.

The skull and crossbones stamp was used by American newspapers to express their indignation at the Act.

PROTEST AGAINST THE STAMP ACT

Colonists in Boston burning the Stamp Act.

The Federal Hall, New York, where the Stamp Act Congress was held.

When news of the Stamp Act reached the colonies, protests broke out.

It wasn't just that goods were going to cost more; it made Americans realize how little control they had over their lives. Politicians far away in Britain were making the decisions, not the American people themselves.

PROTESTS IN BOSTON

Protests against the Stamp Act broke out in towns throughout the colonies. In Boston, Massachusetts, violent protests were aimed at supporters of the Stamp Act. On August 14, 1765, effigies of two men were hung from the Liberty Tree—an elm tree near Boston Common. One **effigy** was of Andrew Oliver, a rich Boston merchant who was the stamp master, or tax collector, for Massachusetts. The other was of Prime Minister Grenville, the head of the British government.

British Prime Minister George Grenville.

Bostonians tarring and feathering a tax collector.

A SIGNIFICANT VICTORY

The chief justice of Boston, Thomas Hutchinson, ordered the effigies to be cut down, but a crowd stopped it from happening. That night, Oliver's effigy was carried by a mob to a building thought to be the headquarters for collecting the Stamp Tax money. They tore down the building, then made their way to Oliver's house. The mob broke in and ransacked the place. The next day, Oliver resigned as stamp master.

SONS OF LIBERTY

To work as well as they did, the protests needed to be well organized. Starting in New York the protest organizers called themselves the Sons of Liberty. The idea spread, and Sons of Liberty groups sprang up in other colonies. Soon stamp masters in Rhode Island, New Hampshire, Pennsylvania, Delaware, Virginia, Connecticut, Maryland, and North Carolina had all resigned from their jobs.

THE STAMP ACT CONGRESS

In October 1765, the Stamp Act Congress was held in New York City. Representatives from nine of the thirteen colonies attended. They called on Britain to abolish the Stamp Act and said it was the colonies, not Britain, who should decide what taxes to pay. Britain took no notice, and on November 1, 1765, the Stamp Act became law.

New York stamp master Cadwallader Colden.

PROTEST IN NEW YORK CITY

On the first day of the new tax, there was a protest in New York City. Just as in Boston, effigies were made. One was of the Devil, the other of Cadwallader Colden, the New York stamp master. Colden tried to calm the crowd, but it wouldn't listen. The crowd set fire to a building he owned, burning his carriages to ash. Colden, like the stamp masters in other colonies, resigned.

REPEAL OF THE STAMP ACT

The boycott of Britain's goods was hurting the British economy, and British politicians feared that foreign powers might take advantage of increasing disorder in the colonies. In March 1766, British politicians agreed to **repeal** the Stamp Act.

A contemporary engraving satirizes the repeal of the Stamp Act by showing it as a funeral procession.

END OF THE PROTESTS

Now that the Stamp Act had been repealed, there was no longer any need for protests, so the Sons of Liberty disbanded and American merchants started trading with Britain again.

But the colonies had taken on Britain and won. They'd shown their determination to go their own way over taxation. It was a sign of what was to come.

9

MASSACRE IN BOSTON

The Stamp Tax had been a complete failure for Britain. However, there was a new British government and it planned to tax the colonies.

In May 1767, Britain introduced the Townshend Duties, which were named after the British politician responsible for them. The new tax meant that glass, wine, china, lead, printing ink, paper, and tea all started to cost more.

BOSTON LEADS

As with the Stamp Act protests, Boston led the way by calling for a new boycott of British goods. This time, it wasn't only merchants who stopped trading with Britain—ordinary Americans stopped buying British goods in stores and British tea was no longer served at home.

British ships arriving in Boston Harbor.

NO TAXATION WITHOUT REPRESENTATION

The colonies saw the Townshend Duties as another example of British interference. Once again they started to protest, and Sons of Liberty groups sprang up. A powerful slogan spread throughout the colonies—"No taxation without representation." It meant the colonies would not allow Britain to force a tax on them. Only taxes imposed by colonial assemblies, which were elected by the Americans themselves, would be acceptable.

BRITAIN RETALIATES

The British warship HMS *Romney* sailed into Boston Harbor in June 1768. That night, mobs took to the streets. British officials fled to a nearby British fort. Britain had lost control of Boston, the most important port in the colonies. It responded by sending in the army. A force of 600 soldiers arrived in Boston in September 1768.

TENSION INCREASES

The presence of the British soldiers—known as "redcoats" because of their red uniforms—angered the people of Boston. Then, in February 1770, Samuel Adams gave a speech at the funeral of Christopher Snider (or Seider), a boy who had been shot during a riot. Although he'd not been killed by the British, Adams convinced the crowd that the British were ultimately to blame.

SAMUEL ADAMS (1722–1803)

Adams was a leading member of the anti-British protest movement. He helped to plan the Stamp Act protests, the Boston Tea Party, and other protests against Britain. Adams was a skillful speaker and was able to convince people that protesting against Britain was the right thing to do. He was one of the Founding Fathers (see below right), and went on to become governor of Massachusetts.

REPEAL OF THE TOWNSHEND DUTIES

Britain had hoped the Townshend Duties would raise a large amount of tax money in the colonies. In fact very little money had come from the tax. Worse still, it had caused widespread protests, a boycott of British goods, and the deaths of innocent people. Britain was forced to think again and on the very day of the Boston Massacre, the Townshend Duties were scrapped. That is, except for tea, which the British still intended to tax.

THE FOUNDING FATHERS

Many years after the **Revolution**, the men who had led the struggle for American **independence** became known as the "Founding Fathers" of the nation. They included the men who had signed the Declaration of Independence in 1776, who led armies in the Revolutionary War, and who wrote the **Constitution** in 1787.

THE BOSTON MASSACRE

On the night of March 5, 1770, Private Hugh White, a guard on duty outside Boston's custom house, was surrounded by a jeering crowd. He reacted by hitting one of them with his musket. The crowd grew larger, and eight redcoats came to rescue White. A redcoat fired into the crowd, possibly by accident, and the people panicked. In the chaos that followed, five men were killed. Samuel Adams later described the event as a massacre.

One of those killed in the massacre was Crispus Attucks, a man of mixed African and Native American descent. He may have been a runaway **slave**.

A particular Account of the most barbarous and

HORRID MASSACRE!

Committed in King-Street, Boston, on Monday, March 5, 1770, by the Soldiery quartered in said

A contemporary newssheet reporting on the massacre.

THE BOSTON TEA PARTY

THE EAST INDIA COMPANY

This major British company traded goods to and from India and Southeast Asia—the area where tea came from. It had money problems and in 1773 the government agreed to help.

After the scrapping of tax on everyday goods, the colonies began to trade with Britain once again.

For a short time the colonies prospered. However, there was still a tax to pay on tea brought to the colonies by British ships. The Americans were big tea drinkers, and as British tea was expensive, merchants smuggled in cheaper Dutch tea.

Lord North, the British prime minister at the time of the Boston Tea Party.

The East India Company used fast modern sailing ships to carry tea around the globe.

CHEAP TEA

The British government gave the East India Company permission to take tons of tea straight to the colonies. (Before this, the company had had to sell its tea to middlemen in London, who added on a profit for themselves before selling it on to American merchants.) Better still, the government scrapped the tax the company had to pay on tea trading.

As a result, the East India Company could sell tea to the colonies at really low prices. Americans would still have to pay a small tax on it, but even so, it would work out cheaper than the smuggled Dutch tea.

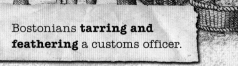

Bostonians **tarring and feathering** a customs officer.

THE COLONIES' REACTION

To the British, it seemed like a safe plan. The price of tea would fall, which would please the Americans. The East India Company would earn money, and the government would receive money from tax.

Instead, American merchants saw it as an attack on their businesses. The East India Company got to choose who could buy its tea directly, and other merchants then had to buy from these middlemen. The tea tax was seen as helping Britain give the Company and its agents total control of the tea trade.

This cartoon shows Lord North forcing tea into the mouth of a woman who represents America.

RESISTANCE

Newspapers and **pamphlets** attacked the plan and when cheap tea arrived at New York and Philadelphia, it was sent straight back to Britain. Tea agents—the men who had the job of actually selling the tea—were threatened, and one by one they all resigned.

Thomas Hutchinson, governor of Massachusetts.

BLOCKADED TEA

On November 28, 1773, an East India Company ship sailed into Boston Harbor. On board the *Dartmouth* were 114 chests of tea. Thomas Hutchinson, governor of Massachusetts, was determined to allow the tea to be brought ashore, but the people of Boston had other ideas. Day after day, thousands came to the harbor to prevent the tea from being landed. Two more tea ships arrived—the *Eleanor* and the *Beaver*. The protestors also stopped them from unloading their tea.

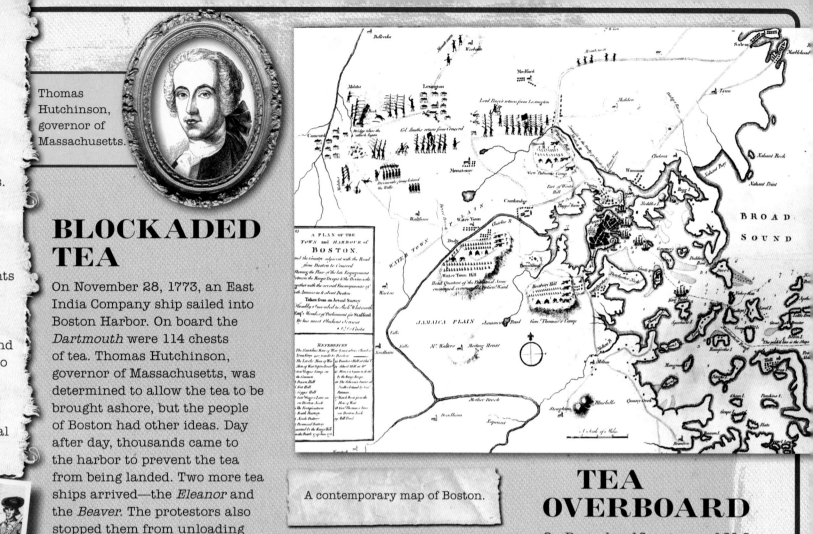

A contemporary map of Boston.

The Boston Tea Party.

TEA OVERBOARD

On December 16, a group of 60 Sons of Liberty, under the direction of Samuel Adams, took the protest further. Disguised as Mohawks (a Native American people), they boarded the three ships and threw 342 chests of tea into the sea. A large crowd of protestors watched from the shore, as did British soldiers who did nothing to stop the Sons.

Many years after the destruction of the tea in Boston Harbor, the incident was given the name by which it is now known—the Boston Tea Party.

OPEN REBELLION

THE FIRST CONTINENTAL CONGRESS

In September 1774, twelve of the thirteen colonies sent representatives to Philadelphia to attend the First Continental Congress. Only Georgia stayed away. They were there to discuss "the present unhappy state of the colonies."

After seven weeks of discussions, the colonies agreed to support the views of the **Patriots**. They called on Britain to repeal the Coercive Acts and to withdraw British troops from Boston. British goods were to be boycotted until these demands had been met, and no goods would be sent from the colonies to Britain.

In Britain, there was an angry reaction to the Boston Tea Party. The prime minister, Lord North, said: "We must control them [the colonies] or submit to them."

There was a growing feeling that Britain had let the colonies get away with too much for too long. The government decided to take tough action.

BOSTON IS PUNISHED

Britain held Massachusetts responsible for encouraging the other colonies to protest. In 1774, the British government brought in laws designed to punish Boston. The colonies named these the Coercive Acts, or the Intolerable Acts.

From June 1, 1774, the port of Boston was to be closed until the tea destroyed by the Boston Tea Party was paid for (it was valued at about £10,000). Worse still, public meetings were banned, and Massachusetts colony was placed under British army rule.

REACTION IN AMERICA

Meetings were held throughout the colonies. People spoke out against Britain. Newspapers and pamphlets defended the rights of the colonies, saying that Britain was attacking their freedom.

An engraving showing the people of Boston as being literally caged by the Intolerable Acts. The men in the rowboat represent other American colonies, offering the Bostonians aid.

one famous speech, Patrick Henry said:

The distinctions between Virginians, ennsylvanians, New Yorkers, and New nglanders are no more. I am not a irginian, but an American!"

REACTION IN BRITAIN

There was an angry reaction in Britain. King George III told Prime Minister North:
"The New England governments are in a state of rebellion, blows must decide whether they are to be subject to this country or independent." General Gage had asked for 20,000 extra troops, but Britain only sent 4,000. In March 1775, General Gage was ordered to end the rebellion in Massachusetts and arrest those responsible for it.

Patrick Henry speaking to the House of Burgesses, the elected body that governed Virginia.

GENERAL THOMAS GAGE (*CA.*1719–1787)

Thomas Gage was **commander in chief** of the British army in North America. After the Boston Tea Party, he was appointed governor of Massachusetts. He told King George III that the Americans "will undoubtedly prove very meek." But in 1775, Gage attempted to seize weapons from American militiamen, and that led to the first shots in the Revolutionary War.

PATRICK HENRY (1736–1799)

Patrick Henry was one of the Founding Fathers of the United States and went on to become governor of Virginia. In 1775, when the colonies were planning their course of action against Britain, Henry gave a famous speech in which he said: "The war is actually begun! The next gale that sweeps from the north will bring to our ears the clash of resounding arms! … Give me liberty, or give me death!"

THE SHOT HEARD 'ROUND THE WORLD

A contemporary map show[ing] **siege** of Boston.

On April 14, 1775, General Gage received orders from Britain to end the rebellion in Massachusetts. He was told to use whatever force was necessary to restore British control. It was the signal for war to begin.

Four days later, General Gage ordered 700 British soldiers to march to Concord, about 16 miles west of Boston. Their orders were to seize weapons and gunpowder, and arrest Patriot (see below right) leaders Samuel Adams and John Hancock. It was to be a secret mission, carried out at night.

Patriot Paul Revere

Paul Revere riding to Lexington.

THE PATRIOTS ARE WARNED

Americans who were prepared to resist the British by force were known as Patriots. As British troops got ready to march, Patriot spies realized something was happening. Three Boston citizens, Paul Revere, William Dawes, and Dr. Samuel Prescott, rode into the countryside to warn fellow Patriots. Revere went to the village of Lexington. He arrived at about midnight and warned Adams and Hancock, who were hiding there. Patriots with muskets rushed to Lexington. They were known as **minutemen** because they had pledged to be ready for battle at a minute's notice.

The Battle of Lexington.

BATTLE OF LEXINGTON

dawn on April 19, British troops ached Lexington on their ay to Concord. They were et by about 70 minutemen termined to stop them from ing any farther. The British dered the Patriots to lay down eir arms, but they refused. A ot rang out. No one knows which le fired first, but there is no ubt about what happened ext. Each side fired at the her, and within minutes ght Patriots were ad. Only one British ldier was wounded. lams and Hancock caped, and the British ntinued on to Concord.

A modern statue of a minuteman in Concord, MA.

The British retreat from Concord.

BATTLE OF CONCORD

The British searched Concord for weapons and gunpowder and destroyed what they found. They then began the long march back to Boston. Just outside Concord, at the North Bridge, minutemen opened fire on them. The British fought off the attack, but three of them were killed. They **retreated** to Boston, fired on all the way by Patriots. It was evening when they reached the safety of Boston. The British had lost 73 men, the Patriots 49.

Within a few days of the battle, thousands of Patriots made their way to the countryside around Boston. The British were trapped inside the city, and a long siege began.

BRITISH STRONGHOLDS CAPTURED

The battles of Lexington and Concord were a rallying call to Patriots. Two of them—Benedict Arnold and Ethan Allen—had the same idea: capture British guns, cannon, and ammunition. They combined their militias and in May 1775 captured the British strongholds of Fort Ticonderoga and Crown Point. More than 100 cannon were seized and taken to the Patriots besieging Boston.

A contemporary pistol.

THE SHOT

Years later, American poet Ralph Waldo Emerson described the first shot fired by the Patriots at Concord as "the shot heard 'round the world."

PATRIOTS & AND & LOYALISTS

★ ★ ★ ★ ★ ★ ★

Patriots: Those who were anti-British and who rebelled against Britain. Also known as Rebels, Revolutionaries, Congress-Men, or American Whigs.

Loyalists: Those who were pro-British and remained on the side of Britain. Also known as Tories or King's Men.

SECOND CONTINENTAL CONGRESS

THE CONTINENTAL ARMY

Because fighting had already begun, the first task of the Congress was to organize an army and appoint a commander. It was known as the Continental Army and the commander in chief was George Washington (Virginia). Each colony was asked to recruit enough men to make the new army about 20,000 strong.

At the start of the war, the British army was well organized, but the Patriot militias were not.

Instead of acting as one combined force, the Patriots acted as many small, local forces. They needed to be brought together to create a united army.

Independence Hall in Philadelphia, where the Congress was held.

GEORGE WASHINGTON (1732–1799)

George Washington was an experienced soldier who had served in the British army during the French and Indian War. He was a natural leader and rose to the rank of colonel. As commander of the Continental Army, his job was to recruit men, train them to become soldiers, and lead the army. After the war, he was elected the first president of the United States of America.

GOVERNMENT OF ALL THE COLONIES

In May 1775, the Second Continental Congress met in Philadelphia. This time all thirteen colonies sent representatives. Most had attended the first Congress the year before, but there were some new faces at this meeting, including Thomas Jefferson (Virginia) and Benjamin Franklin (Pennsylvania). For the next six years, the Continental Congress was the central government of all the colonies.

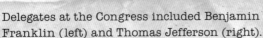

Delegates at the Congress included Benjamin Franklin (left) and Thomas Jefferson (right).

BATTLE OF BUNKER HILL

After the battles at Lexington and Concord, the British army was trapped in Boston, besieged by thousands of Patriots. Thinking the Patriots were about to bombard Boston from nearby hills, the British launched an attack. It took place on June 17, 1775, on Breed's Hill. Oddly, the battle is known as the battle of Bunker Hill, the hill behind Breed's Hill.

Boston was woken by the roar of guns fired at Patriot defenses by British warship HMS *Lively*. Soon, **redcoats** were advancing up Breed's Hill and the nearby town of Charlestown was set on fire. Patriots fought off the British twice, until they ran out of ammunition. But they couldn't hold off the British a third time and were defeated. The battle of Bunker Hill was the bloodiest battle of the whole war, with about 226 Britons and 140 Patriots killed.

BRITISH WARSHIPS IN BOSTON HARBOR

THE OLIVE BRANCH PETITION

Some of the representatives at the Congress wanted to end the conflict quickly and peacefully, before the fighting got any worse. In July 1775, the Olive Branch Petition was sent to King George III. It asked him not to fight the colonies, but to listen to their concerns. The king refused to read the petition. Instead, on August 23, 1775, he declared the colonies to be in open rebellion against Britain. It was nothing less than a declaration of war by Britain against its colonies in North America.

British redcoats at the battle of Bunker Hill.

DECLARATION OF INDEPENDENCE

THOMAS PAINE'S COMMON SENSE

In January 1776, a pamphlet was published called *Common Sense: Addressed to the Inhabitants of America*. The author was Thomas Paine, an Englishman who had lived in America for little more than a year. Paine had taken the side of the Patriots and his pamphlet captured their mood. Written in language that everyone could understand, it called King George III "the royal brute" and called on Americans to break with Britain.

Despite the British victory at Bunker Hill, the British army was still trapped inside Boston.

The siege dragged on for a whole year until, in March 1776, the British army **evacuated** the town. The British sailed away to Canada, leaving Boston and the thirteen colonies on their own.

FREE AND INDEPENDENT STATES

Declaring independence was a huge step to take. It could only be done by Congress, and only if it was what the colonies wanted. In May 1776, Virginia became the first colony to push for independence, if Congress decided to discuss it. Other colonies instructed their congressmen to vote in favor. However, Pennsylvania, Delaware, New Jersey, New York, and Maryland instructed their representatives to vote no.

TOWARD INDEPENDENCE

By early 1776, the colonies were talking of independence. The Continental Congress was acting as central government and links were being made with countries overseas. The colonies were issuing money, with the American dollar replacing the British pound. Samuel Adams summed it up when he said: "Is not America already independent? Why then not declare it?"

The draft Declaration of Independence is presented to Congress.

VOTING FOR INDEPENDENCE

Richard Henry Lee (Virginia) proposed that Congress accept the colonies were "free and independent states." Congress set up a committee to draft a declaration based on Lee's proposal. Most of the drafting work was done by Thomas Jefferson (Virginia) and on July 1, Congress discussed it. At the vote, nine colonies were in favor of independence; four were against. This was no good, so it was discussed again the next day. This time, twelve of the thirteen colonies voted for independence. New York didn't vote either way, but a week later said it was in favor.

Richard Henry Lee

THOMAS JEFFERSON (1743–1826)

Born to a wealthy farming family in Virginia, Thomas Jefferson became a lawyer and then a politician. He was chosen to draft the Declaration of Independence because of his skill with words. Years later, he said he wanted it to be "an expression of the American mind." It marked the birth of the United States of America. Jefferson went on to become the new nation's third president.

A NEW FLAG

In 1777, Congress adopted a flag for the new United States. It had thirteen red and white stripes and thirteen stars on a blue background—a star for each state.

DECLARATION OF INDEPENDENCE

On July 4, 1776, Congress adopted the Declaration of Independence. Copies were printed and sent to every colony. It was read at public meetings, so everyone knew what was happening. The colonies were breaking away from Britain and the United States of America was in the making.

BRITISH FORCES

The British army in North America was a typical European fighting force.

Its troops were trained, disciplined, organized, and well equipped. Above all, many of the soldiers were experienced fighting men who had seen action.

BRITISH REDCOATS

The red-coated regulars were the backbone of the army. These men had joined for life, which in practice meant 25 years. Then there were the **enlisted** men—those who had answered the call to join the army for the war. Most soldiers came from the lowest levels of British society, and many were from Scotland and Ireland, not England. Officers came from the aristocracy (the upper class) and the gentry (families who owned a lot of land and had good positions in society).

Army coats were red—not to hide the sight of blood, but so that soldiers could identify each other on the battlefield through the thick smoke of gunfire.

AMERICAN LOYALISTS

Many Americans remained loyal to Britain and fought on the British side. Some joined Loyalist regiments that were part of the British army. For example, the King's Royal Regiment was created by Loyalist refugees who had fled to Canada. Another Loyalist regiment was the Caledonian **Volunteers**, made up of Scottish settlers. In addition, there were groups of American militia, commanded by British officers.

BLACK LOYALISTS

Thousands of African-Americans fought with the British. Many were escaped slaves, and in return for their military service the British promised them their freedom. Lord Dunmore, governor of Virginia, called for slaves to leave their Patriot masters and join his Ethiopian Regiment. He offered to free them from slavery, and 800 men joined his black-only regiment.

The Black Pioneers were an offshoot of the Ethiopian Regiment. They carried out laboring duties such as road building, which freed other soldiers for combat duty.

Hessian soldiers surrender to General Washington.

GERMAN MERCENARIES

About one-third of all British forces were **mercenaries**—some 30,000 men. They were conscripted (forcibly taken) into the British army, then paid to fight the Americans. Most came from the Hesse region of Germany and were known as **Hessians**. They made good soldiers and arrived in regiments ready to fight. Some Hessians **deserted** in return for land (50 acres a man), but most stayed loyal to Britain.

Hessian soldiers were made to leave their homes and fight for the British in America.

Thayendanegea, one of the Mohawks who fought for the British.

NATIVE AMERICANS

Native Americans feared they would lose their land to settlers if America gained independence from Britain. For this reason, many took Britain's side in the war. A notable example was Thayendanegea or Joseph Brant, who led Loyalist Mohawk forces in battles along the Canadian–American border.

MUSKET AND BAYONET

The standard redcoat weapon was the Long Land Pattern musket, known by the troops as the Brown Bess. It was 62½ inches long, and even longer when its stabbing **bayonet** was in place. It fired one shot at a time—a ball of solid lead—and then had to be reloaded. Troops were expected to fire four rounds per minute, though two to three was more usual. It was usually fired in a mass volley at about 50 yards, then followed by a bayonet charge.

REVOLUTIONARY FORCES

George Washington became commander in chief of the Continental Army in 1775.

He wanted to create a disciplined army, trained to fire musket volleys and advance in line with bayonets fixed. It was to be similar to the British and other armies of Europe—but first he had to recruit the soldiers.

Washington takes command of the troops.

THE CONTINENTAL ARMY

Congress wanted to recruit 20,000 men to form the Continental Army. To do this, each of the thirteen colonies was asked to provide a set number of men. Some were little more than boys, as the minimum age was 16, or 15 if parents gave permission. It was to be a full-time army, with soldiers enlisting for three years or for the duration of the war.

Troops were to wear a standard-issue uniform. Infantry wore blue coats lined with white fabric, and the artillery wore blue coats lined with red. However, as fabric supplies were scarce, many soldiers wore their own clothes.

MILITIAS AND MINUTEMEN

The Continental Army did not exist at the start of the war. Instead, each colony had its own force of part-time citizen soldiers known as a militia. It was their duty to defend the colony. They were expected to provide their own weapons and uniforms, though many simply wore their everyday work clothes.

In the early stages of the war, some militiamen formed themselves into elite companies. These keen young Patriots said that they would be ready to fight at a minute's notice. The minutemen, as they were known, saw action in the first battles of the war. But, as the war progressed, the minutemen companies were merged back into the regular militias.

A minuteman in uniform.

ntinental
my
icers
aring a
riety of
iforms.

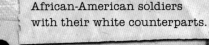

African-American soldiers with their white counterparts.

African-American Peter Salem is credited with shooting British Major Pitcairn at the battle of Bunker Hill.

BLACK PATRIOTS

Not enough volunteers joined the Continental Army, so African-American slaves and freemen were allowed to enter its ranks. It is thought that about 5,000 fought as Patriots, whereas 20,000 fought with the British. Slaves were offered their freedom in return for joining the army. For example, in 1778, Rhode Island enlisted slaves and freemen into the 1st Rhode Island Regiment. Even though it had many white soldiers, it was known as the Black Regiment. About 88 slaves joined its ranks, and all were given their freedom.

A recruiting poster for Washington's army.

NATIVE AMERICANS

At first, Native Americans tried to stay out of the war. An Oneida leader said: "We are unwilling to join either side of such a contest, for we love you both, Old England and New. Should the Great King of England apply to us for aid, we should deny him—and should the colonies apply, we shall refuse." But it was impossible to remain **neutral** for long, and Native Americans did indeed take sides. Most sided with the British, but the Oneidas, Tuscaroras, Catawbas, and Mohicans gave their support to the Americans.

FLINTLOCK MUSKET

The standard weapon for an infantryman was a flintlock musket. There were 13 steps to firing it. He had to get a cartridge, tear it open with his teeth, put a little bit of gunpowder in the firing mechanism, put the rest of the powder and a lead ball down the barrel, ram the ball and powder home, cock the musket, and fire. A soldier was expected to fire a shot every 20 seconds.

Modern military reenactors dressed as minutemen.

BRITISH VICTORIES

The British army left Boston in spring 1776. For a short time it appeared that Britain had abandoned its American colonies.

In truth, Britain had no intention of cutting the colonies adrift. Instead, a full-scale British assault was secretly planned for later that year.

The British leave Boston.

THE BRITISH PLAN

A secret plan was worked out. The British army, led by commander in chief General William Howe, would mount a massive expedition to take back control of the colonies. The assault was to come from the sea, with thousands of troops landing on Staten Island and then marching on to capture New York. Howe hoped to lure George Washington into battle, defeat him, and then negotiate a peaceful end to the war.

WASHINGTON DIGS IN

British forces landed on Staten Island on July 2, 1776. Some 10,000 redcoats made camp and then waited. Troops continued to arrive, and by August Howe had a force of 32,000. Washington was outnumbered. With only 20,000 men, many of whom were poorly equipped and not fully trained, it would have been best to abandon New York. But that would have been bad for **morale**, so he decided to stay and fight.

The Battle of Long Island.

THE BATTLE OF LONG ISLAND

On August 27, the British stormed Washington's positions, which quickly collapsed. The Patriots lost about 300 men, the British fewer than 100. It was a decisive British victory—but it was also a lost opportunity. Had the British continued to fight, it might have forced Washington to surrender. Instead, under cover of fog, Washington withdrew his troops. The war was set to continue.

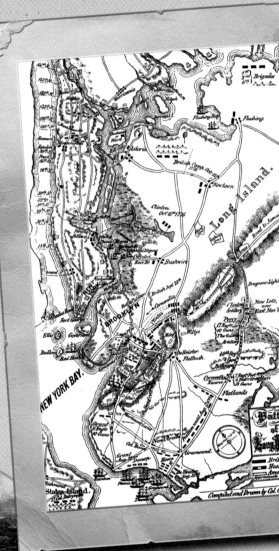

A contemporary map showing the battle.

GENERAL WILLIAM HOWE (1729–1814)

William Howe was a second cousin of King George III. He fought with success in the French and Indian War and replaced General Thomas Gage as commander in chief of the British army in North America. Although he had chances to defeat George Washington once and for all, Howe felt he had accomplished his mission by regaining Manhattan Island.

NEW YORK CITY BURNS

British redcoats marched in triumph through New York City. Loyalists cheered and turned on their Patriot neighbors. On September 21, fire broke out, destroying about a quarter of the city. Patriot fire starters were suspected. The partly ruined city remained in British hands for the rest of the war.

This contemporary cartoon shows the British crowing about their victory.

News from America, or the Patriots in the Dumps.

AMERICAN PRISONERS

Howe returned to Manhattan, and British forces captured Fort Washington. Thousands of prisoners captured at White Plains and Fort Washington were taken to New York City, where they were kept in makeshift jails and rotting ships in the harbor.

British warships forcing a passage up the Hudson River.

CAPTURE OF FORT WASHINGTON

For the next few weeks, Howe did very little. Washington took full advantage and in mid-October he retreated from Manhattan Island, leaving some 3,000 men to hold Fort Washington. The British eventually gave chase. On October 28, at the Battle of White Plains, British troops scored another victory, sending Washington and the Continental Army into full retreat across New Jersey.

"THE GAME IS PRETTY NEAR UP"

WASHINGTON STRIKES BACK

On Christmas Day 1776, Washington led some 2,400 Continentals back across the icy Delaware River. Men, horses, and cannon weighed down the little boats, and it took nine hours before last of the army was safely on the New Jersey side. From there they marched nine miles to Trenton, where a force of Hessians was station Bloody footprints were left in the snow, as son men's feet were wrapped only in rags.

In early December 1776, General Washington and the Continental Army retreated across the Delaware River into Pennsylvania.

Thinking the cause was lost, many soldiers gave up and went home, leaving the army with only about 3,000 men. Elsewhere, thousands of Patriots took up the offer of a **pardon** from King George III, in return for their loyalty. Washington was crestfallen, and in a letter he wrote: "I think the game is pretty near up."

BREATHING SPACE

With the British in their winter quarters in New York City, Washington was able to regroup the Continental Army. As Christmas approached, its strength doubled to about 6,000 men. It was time for Washington to take the fight to the British.

SAVED BY THE WINTER

Philadelphia, the headquarters of the Continental Congress, was an obvious target for the British. Capturing Philadelphia would have dealt a crushing blow to the leaders of the Revolution. British troops reached the wintry Delaware River. Fearing they were about to cross, the Continental Congress moved out to Baltimore. But, instead of pursing Washington's ragtag army, General Howe decided the British should return to New York City and spend the winter there.

Washington crossing the Delaware.

MERCENARIES CAPTURED

In a surprise attack on December 26, the German mercenaries were overwhelmed and about 1,000 taken prisoner. Washington took them back across the Delaware River to Philadelphia, where they were paraded through the streets, almost causing a riot among the townsfolk.

Captured Hessians marching behind George Washington.

BATTLE OF PRINCETON

Three days later, on January 3, 1777, Washington outmaneuvered British General Charles Cornwallis, who hoped to do battle with him at Trenton. Instead, Washington captured the British-held town of Princeton and seized supplies left by Cornwallis.

Washington could now give his troops their winter rest, knowing his men's spirits had been lifted by their successes at Trenton and Princeton. The army headed north to **winter quarters** in Morristown.

MORALE BOOST

The victory at Trenton boosted the morale of Washington's men, but now he faced a problem. The men had the option of quitting the army on the last day of the year. Washington couldn't allow that to happen, and on December 29 he led them back over the Delaware River. On December 31 he appealed to the men: "Stay for just six more weeks for an extra bounty of $10." It worked, and the army stood by their leader.

❧ REACTION ❧ IN BRITAIN

★ ★ ★ ★ ★ ★

News of Washington's success at Trenton came as a shock to the British government, who had thought the Patriots were close to total defeat. Now, though, came the possibility that the Patriots would fight back. Worse still was the prospect that France, Britain's old enemy, would get involved.

The Hessians surrender at Trenton.

SARATOGA, THE TURNING POINT

Despite the setbacks at Trenton and Princeton, the British were still confident of winning the war.

General John Burgoyne, commander of the British army in Canada, was so sure of success he said Britain would win by Christmas 1777. In fact, "Gentleman Johnny," as he was known, led the redcoats to a crushing defeat.

TARGET PHILADELPHIA

In July 1777, after months of little action by either side, British forces set out on a mission to capture Philadelphia, the American capital. But instead of marching the 40 miles overland from their base at New York (the shortest route), General Howe sent his 15,000 men by sea. It took 260 troop ships six long weeks to sail south down the coasts of New Jersey and Delaware. When they arrived at the head of Chesapeake Bay, Maryland, the men were tired and short of provisions.

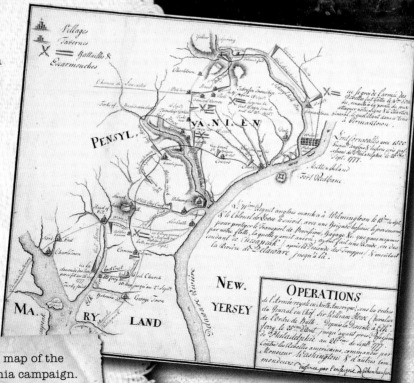

A Hessian map of the Philadelphia campaign.

The Battle of Germantown, part of the Philadelphia campaign.

BATTLE OF BRANDYWINE

The British marched north to Philadelphia, but General Washington and 11,000 Patriots were waiting for them at Brandywine Creek. On September 11, the British attacked. Washington was caught off guard and forced to retreat. Realizing that Philadelphia was about to fall, the Continental Congress moved out to Lancaster and then to York, Pennsylvania. On September 26, the British took Philadelphia.

30

BURGOYNE ON THE MARCH

At the same time as General Howe was fighting his way to Philadelphia, the British army in Canada was on the move. General Burgoyne's plan was to take a force of 8,000 troops south to join up with General Howe's army.

Burgoyne recaptured Fort Ticonderoga, then continued south through difficult terrain. Patriot **militias** attacked him all the way, slowing him down. Reinforcements never arrived.

BATTLE OF SARATOGA

Burgoyne could have returned to the safety of Fort Ticonderoga, but he chose to carry on south. The British met with fierce opposition from Patriots. By October, Burgoyne's army was trapped at Saratoga, New York, surrounded by the Continental army led by General Horatio Gates. On October 14, Burgoyne surrendered and 6,000 redcoats became prisoners of war. This was the first major victory for the Patriots and marked a turning point in the war.

GENERAL HORATIO GATES (1727–1806)

Born in Britain, Horatio Gates served with the British army in North America during the French and Indian War. After that war he left the army and settled in America. When the Revolutionary War began, he offered his services to General Washington. Following his success at Saratoga, there were calls for Gates to replace Washington as commander in chief, but Congress backed Washington.

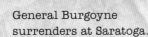

General Burgoyne surrenders at Saratoga.

THE DEATH OF JANE McCREA (1752–77)

In July 1777, a group of Native Americans from Burgoyne's army attacked a settlers' farm. Some of the family were killed, and Jane McCrea was taken prisoner. The plan was to trade her for a reward from the British, but it went wrong. She was killed and scalped. Burgoyne demanded that the culprits be handed over to the British, but the Native Americans refused, and most left the British army.

RIFLEMAN TIMOTHY MURPHY (1751–1818)

At the Battle of Bemis Heights, October 7, 1777, Patriot rifleman Timothy Murphy fired four shots from 300 yards, killing Sir Francis Clerke and General Simon Fraser. He was an expert marksman, and today we would describe him as a sniper.

"A DREARY KIND OF PLACE"

George Washington at Valley Forge.

The final battle of 1777 was fought at Whitemarsh, Pennsylvania.

Here, in the first week of December, General Washington's troops fought off the British in a series of **skirmishes**. The British stopped their attack and returned to winter quarters in Philadelphia. The Continental Army also withdrew and after an eight-day march reached their winter camp at Valley Forge.

SEASONAL FIGHTING

There was an understanding among the armies of the time that battles were fought according to the seasons. In Europe, the fighting seasons were spring, summer, and fall. Armies never fought battles during the winter, when the weather was at its worst and there were fewer hours of daylight.

The march to Valley Forge.

VALLEY FORGE WINTER CAMP

The Revolutionary War followed the seasons. However, General Washington was prepared to "break the rules," as he did in the winter battles of Trenton and Princeton. But, as neither side could fight all year round, they eventually hunkered down in their winter quarters. For the British, their camp during the winter of 1777–78 was in the comfort and warmth of New York and Philadelphia. For Washington and the Continental Army, it was Valley Forge, 25 miles northwest of Philadelphia. Washington described it as a "dreary kind of place and uncomfortably provided."

CAMP CONDITIONS

Washington chose Valley Forge because it was on high ground he could defend. It was also only a day's ride from Philadelphia—close enough for him to keep an eye on the occupying British. A few days before Christmas 1777, the army of 12,000 men arrived. They set about constructing timber huts and fortifications, turning Valley Forge into the second largest city in North America.

KILLER DISEASES

The army was ravaged by sickness and disease. Typhoid, jaundice, dysentery, and pneumonia killed about 2,500 men that winter at Valley Forge. Washington remembered his wife, Martha, describing how to inoculate against disease. He ordered his medics to create small wounds in healthy soldiers' arms. Pus from soldiers infected with smallpox was rubbed into the wounds, inoculating healthy soldiers against catching this killer disease.

Baron von Steuben

READY FOR THE NEW FIGHTING SEASON

In February 1778, Baron Wilhelm von Steuben arrived at Valley Forge. He'd met Benjamin Franklin and had traveled from France to help the Patriot cause. Von Steuben had served with the Prussian army and was an expert in training soldiers. Day after day he **drilled** the Continental Army, and by June 1778 Washington's men were ready to move out from Valley Forge. The new fighting season was about to begin.

DRESSED IN RAGS

Conditions for the men were hard. They lacked suitable clothes and their shoes had fallen apart from marching. They wrapped themselves in rags to keep warm. Wives, daughters, mothers, and sisters came to the camp and did what they could to help. They patched the soldiers' clothes, made shirts, and knit socks.

The army's supply network broke down, and food and medical supplies failed to get through. The men resorted to eating "**firecake**"—a tasteless mixture of flour and water. Faced with these conditions, soldiers deserted. Washington's officers were worried there might even be a mutiny.

Washington riding with his friend, Major General Lafayette.

BARON STEUBEN DRILLING THE TROOPS.

FRANCE JOINS THE WAR

Britain's fears that France, her old enemy, would enter the war were well founded.

The peace treaty the two nations had signed in 1763, at the end of the French and Indian War, had pushed France out of North America. France wanted to strike back at Britain, and the Revolutionary War was a perfect opportunity.

BRITAIN SHOWS WEAKNESS

From far across the Atlantic Ocean, France kept watch on the progress of the war. The early British successes were taken as signs that France was wise not to take sides too soon with the Patriots. But then, in December 1777, France heard the news that British General Burgoyne had surrendered 6,000 redcoats at Saratoga. This was a clear sign that Britain could be beaten.

French ships began to recognize American ships as those of an independent country.

FRANCE HELPS THE PATRIOTS

The Patriots saw France as their friend. Like them, France had good reason to be anti-British. As early as 1775, the Patriot diplomat Benjamin Franklin had been to Paris and asked the French for help. At first, France was reluctant to be drawn into another war against Britain. However, France did agree to help the Patriots, and from the start of the war sent them money, clothes, weapons, and gunpowder in secret.

Benjamin Franklin at the French Court.

French troops in America.

FRANCE RECOGNIZES THE U.S.

In February 1778, France recognized the United States as an independent country. It meant that France would support the Patriots in their struggle against the British. By June 1778, France was sending soldiers to fight alongside the Patriots.

BENJAMIN FRANKLIN (1706–1790)

Born in Boston, Massachusetts, Franklin worked as a printer and scientist, and was also a skilled **diplomat** and statesman. He spoke to the British government against Britain taxing its American colonies. It was Franklin who persuaded France to support the Patriots. He was one of the Founding Fathers of the United States.

BENEDICT ARNOLD (1741–1801)

AMERICAN TRAITOR

Benedict Arnold was born in Connecticut. He was a general in the Continental Army and saw action in many battles. In 1779, he was charged with using government money for his own personal use. Arnold felt he was owed the money as payment for his military service. When he didn't get it, he tried to sell secrets to the British. His plan failed, but Arnold fled the Patriot army and became a general in the British forces. He led British soldiers against his American brothers. After the war he made a new life for himself in Britain.

WAR AT SEA

John Paul Jones, a Scottish sea captain who supported the Patriots, brought the war to the shores of Britain. He captured the British warship HMS *Drake*, attacked ships off the coast of Britain and Ireland, and raided the town of Whitehaven on the northwest coast of England.

In 1779, Jones took command of the *Bonhomme Richard*, an old ship given to the Patriots by France. That September, the *Bonhomme Richard* fought a fierce battle against the 50-gun British warship HMS *Serapis*, off England's east coast. When the British asked Jones to surrender, he called out: "I have not yet begun to fight!" After almost four hours, it was HMS *Serapis* that surrendered, and Jones's words became a battle cry for the Patriot cause.

A naval battle between American and British warships.

THE WAR MOVES SOUTH

As the summer of 1778 approached, the Patriots' position was much improved.

The Continental Army was preparing to leave its winter quarters at Valley Forge, rested and ready to do battle, and reinforcements from France were on the way. As for the British, they had a new commander in chief, General Sir Henry Clinton, who had important orders from London.

Sir Henry Clinton

PHILADELPHIA ABANDONED

Clinton was instructed to concentrate on fighting France. Following his orders, he sent 5,000 troops to attack the French colony of St. Lucia, an island in the Caribbean Sea. He was also ordered to abandon Philadelphia and make New York the British base.

This painting of the Battle of Monmouth includes Molly Pitcher, a woman believed have fought alongside the male soldiers.

THE BATTLE OF MONMOUTH

The British army of 10,000 soldiers began withdrawing from Philadelphia in June 1778. General Washington seized the chance to attack the rear of the long marching **column** of soldiers at Monmouth, New Jersey, but he failed. The Battle of Monmouth was the last of the major battles fought in the northern colonies.

The British marched on to New York. A few days later, French troop ships landed in New Jersey, bringing 4,000 soldiers to fight with the Patriots.

George Washington at the Battle of Monmouth.

THE SOUTHERN COLONIES

In late 1778, Britain turned its attention to the southern colonies. Clinton planned to use them as a base from which to advance north, retaking the lost northern colonies one by one. A force of 3,000 redcoats was sent to Georgia, and the towns of Savannah and Augusta were soon in British hands.

The British treated the Georgians well. As a result, many joined a Loyalist militia, prepared to fight on the British side. In September 1779, Savannah was besieged by 3,500 French and 1,500 Patriot troops. The following month they stormed the town, but the British and Loyalist forces held their ground and the attack failed. The French left, and the Patriots headed up the coast to Charleston.

HIT-AND-RUN TACTICS

Under General Nathanael Greene, commander of the Continental Army in the South, the Patriots began a new type of warfare. Small groups began raiding British positions, taking them by surprise. The British were used to set-piece battles and were unable to respond to these sudden attacks by Patriot fighters.

A small band of soldiers crosses the Pee Dee River to attack the British.

THE SIEGE OF CHARLESTON

Charleston, a major seaport in South Carolina, was the next target for the British. At Christmas 1779, Clinton and a fleet of 90 ships carrying 7,600 redcoats sailed from New York. From February to May 1780, Charleston was under siege. There was no way out for the defending Patriots, and on May 12, Charleston was surrendered to the British. Some 5,000 Patriots were taken prisoner, and 343 cannon, 6,000 muskets, and 376 barrels of gunpowder were seized.

As the British plan to control the southern colonies seemed to be working, General Clinton returned to New York, leaving General Cornwallis heading the campaign in the South.

THE BRITISH IN RETREAT

By 1781, British hopes of controlling the southern colonies had disappeared, and they were left with just Savannah, Charleston, and a remote fort in South Carolina. The war was moving toward its final stage.

The 1779 attack on Savannah.

General Cornwallis became convinced that Virginia held the key to British success.

If the British controlled Virginia, it would drive a wedge between the northern and southern colonies, cutting them off from each other. Cornwallis arrived in Virginia in spring 1781, in command of some 7,200 redcoats.

THE BRITISH PLAN

Cornwallis headed for the Virginia coast, and in August 1781 he began to build a base at Yorktown. From there he'd be able to keep in contact with General Clinton, commander in chief of the British army, based in New York. The plan was for ships to bring supplies and troops, building up a huge British army. When all was ready, Cornwallis would move out from Yorktown and wipe out any Patriot resistance he met.

Cornwallis thought that Yorktown was the ideal place for his base. In fact, it was the worst place to choose. He had his back to the sea, and as long as he couldn't escape by ship, he would be trapped there. General Clinton realized the problem that Cornwallis had made for himself and ordered him to leave. Cornwallis refused, saying that Virginia was too important to lose.

Patriot and British ships fighting off the coast of Virginia.

THE BATTLE OF THE CHESAPEAKE

The British did not know that a fleet of 24 French warships under the command of Admiral François-Joseph-Paul, comte de Grasse, was on its way to America. They arrived off the coast of Virginia. A fleet of nineteen British warships sailed down the coast from New York, and on September 5 the two navies met. The Battle of the Chesapeake was the decisive naval battle of the war. The British navy was defeated, leaving the French in control of the waters around Yorktown.

Meanwhile, General Washington and French General Jean-Baptiste-Donatien de Vimeur, comte de Rochambeau, had joined forces and 16,000 Patriot and French troops marched south from New Jersey. By late September they were at Yorktown. Cornwallis, 7,200 redcoats, and 800 sailors were trapped.

Admiral François-Joseph-Paul, comte de Grasse

A map of the siege of Yorktown.

French General Jean-Baptiste-Donatien de Vimeur, comte de Rochambeau.

THE SIEGE OF YORKTOWN

On October 6, 1781, Washington personally fired the first cannon at the British positions. For the next 11 days, Yorktown was bombarded day and night. On the night of October 16, Cornwallis attempted to escape across the York River, but a storm blew up and he was forced back.

The next morning, October 17, a British drummer boy beat out the signal for a **parley**—a meeting to discuss a **truce**. An officer waving a white handkerchief appeared. The bombardment was halted, officers from each side came together, and a meeting began. The British asked that their soldiers be allowed to return to Britain, rather than become prisoners of war. Washington refused and gave his terms—complete surrender. On October 19, Cornwallis and Washington signed the document of surrender. British troops marched out of Yorktown and laid down their weapons.

Fighting at the Siege of Yorktown.

Cornwallis surrenders to the Patriots.

The Patriot commanders at Yorktown.

GENERAL CHARLES CORNWALLIS (1738–1805)

Charles Cornwallis came from an upper-class English family. As a young man he joined the British army and fought in the Seven Years' War. He was promoted many times, and in the American Revolutionary War he was commander of the British army in the South. Despite his surrender at Yorktown, his army career continued in other parts of the world.

MAKING THE PEACE

The British surrender at Yorktown was a triumph for the Patriots.

However, there was still much to do before Britain finally let go of its North American colonies. Britain still had 30,000 troops in America and was in control of New York, Savannah, and Charleston—what would happen to them? Most of all, the two sides had to come together for peace talks.

TROOPS OUT

British attitudes toward the war had changed, and now all talk was of peace. In April 1782, the British government ordered its troops to leave New York, Savannah, and Charleston. The troops didn't leave straightaway. It was July 1782 before Savannah was evacuated, and Charleston remained in British hands until December. As for New York, which had fallen to the British in 1776, the last of the redcoats didn't leave until November 1783.

This British political cartoon shows the "blessings of peace" as being worth very little to Britain.

This unfinished painting shows Benjamin Franklin and other American diplomats negotiating peace with Britain.

A map of the United States after 1783.

COLONIES BECOME STATES

The Treaty of Paris redrew the map of North America. The boundary between Canada, which Britain retained, and the USA was largely fixed. All land south of the Canadian border down to Florida and west from the Atlantic Ocean to the Mississippi River would belong to the USA. Florida was given to Spain. It was also agreed that prisoners of war on both sides were to be released, and British merchants who were owed money by American traders should be paid. There were to be no more colonies in the U.S. Instead, the original thirteen colonies became the first states in the new United States of America.

Washington arrives in New York to a hero's welcome.

THE TREATY OF PARIS

April 1782 was also the starting point for peace talks. They were held in Paris, the capital of France. America's chief diplomats were Benjamin Franklin, John Adams, Henry Laurens, and John Jay. Britain sent Richard Oswald and David Hartley. The talks lasted for more than a year, but finally, on September 3, 1783, the Treaty of Paris was signed. It marked the official end to the war and recognized the United States of America as a free and independent nation in its own right.

The Treaty of Paris.

GEORGE WASHINGTON ENTERS NEW YORK

With the British gone from New York, General Washington and the Continental Army entered the town at the end of November 1783. On December 4, he called a meeting of his senior officers and announced he was resigning from the army. Washington had done what Congress had asked him to do, and that job was now over. As for his future, he planned to return to his family's **plantation** in Virginia, where he would quietly farm the land growing tobacco, wheat, and corn. However, the United States of America was not about to let the hero of the hour fade away from public life just yet.

AFTER THE WAR

The United States had gained independence from Britain.

The world's newest nation of 4 million people was now on its own, and the hard work of running the country was about to begin. It was no easy task, as the thirteen states were as good as mini-countries, each making its own laws, although there was also a weak central government made up of officials elected by Congress. The system was complicated and confusing. It needed changing.

THE PHILADELPHIA CONVENTION

In the summer of 1787, representatives from twelve states met in Philadelphia. They came together to form a national government of all the states. Rhode Island stayed away, as it saw no reason for the system to change. Each state sent several of its leading speakers to the Philadelphia Convention (also known as the Constitutional Convention). Among the group from Virginia were George Washington and James Madison.

THE ONE-CHAMBER SYSTEM

Madison said the states had too much power. He proposed a national government made up of a single elected body (a one-chamber system). It would be chosen by the people for the people and would have ultimate power over the states. Crucially, the states would be represented according to the sizes of their populations. This last idea was unpopular with smaller states, who felt they would not be well represented in a one-chamber system. They thought they would be giving away power to larger states.

James Madison

THE GREAT COMPROMISE

It looked like the Convention was going to end without an agreement being reached. That was until representatives from Connecticut put forward a compromise to please all the states. Their plan was to have a national government with two branches—a two-chamber system. There would be a Senate and a House of Representatives. Each state would send an equal number of representatives to the Senate and one representative to the House of Representatives for each 30,000 residents of the state.

The signing of the Constitution.

"WE THE PEOPLE..."

The compromise was accepted and the Convention moved on to writing a constitution—a set of rules—for the national government and the nation. The handwritten document began with words that were to become famous the world over: "We the People of the United States ..."

On September 13, 1788, the Constitution was approved by the Continental Congress. The first national government of the United States began work on March 4, 1789, based in New York City.

PRESIDENT GEORGE WASHINGTON

A leader was needed to act as head of the new government. There was only one choice for the job—George Washington. He was elected the first president of the United States, with John Adams as vice president. In a ceremony in New York City on April 30, 1789, Washington was sworn into office. "I greatly fear that my countrymen will expect too much from me," wrote Washington, shortly after becoming president. There certainly was much resting on his shoulders, but under Washington's firm and skillful guidance, the United States of America took its place on the world stage. The rest, as they say, is history.

The inauguration of President George Washington.

IMPACT OF THE WAR ON AMERICA

The American Revolutionary War was a political war.

It was about the American people wanting to govern themselves and not to be ruled by a foreign power. It's hard to know how many people died, but some say that as many as 25,000 Americans and 10,000 Britons gave their lives during the eight years of war.

The tragedy is that it was a war at all, and that the argument between Britain and its colonies could not be settled peacefully. Apart from independence, what impact did the war have on the people of America?

LOYAL EMIGRATION

As many as 500,000 Americans are thought to have remained loyal to Britain throughout the war. Many were farmers, and during the war Loyalists had seen their land and property confiscated. The Treaty of Paris, 1783, which ended the war, protected Loyalists from further persecution. Despite this, thousands decided to emigrate. Up to 100,000 Loyalists left the United States to begin new lives in Britain, Canada, Nova Scotia, and the West Indies. Whatever land and property they left behind was sold off at high prices. Poor working people could not afford it, and it was bought by rich landowners whose fortunes increased as a result.

SLAVERY REMAINED

Before the war, slavery was taken for granted. Even leaders of the Revolution, George Washington and Thomas Jefferson, used slaves on their plantations. Now, with the war over, there was an obvious problem. The Declaration of Independence (1776) stated that "All men are created equal"—yet when the first census was taken in 1790, a total of 694,280 slaves was recorded (about 18 percent of the total population). The war opened people's eyes to the question of slavery. It became a major issue between the states, divided society, and led to the American Civil War of 1861–65.

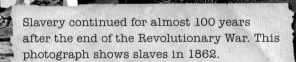
Slavery continued for almost 100 years after the end of the Revolutionary War. This photograph shows slaves in 1862.

A FAIRER SOCIETY?

American society changed after the war. It became easier for men from humble origins to have their say. They believed that in the new United States of America they had as much right to be heard as the men from leading families and those who were wealthy. American society had the chance to become fairer for all people, regardless of their background. However, many inequalities remained long into the future.

Washington supervising agricultural work at his Mount Vernon estate.

A soldier fires on a Native American scout.

IMPACT ON NATIVE AMERICANS

Native Americans had feared all along that they would lose land if America won the war. Their fears were well founded, and white settlers moved west onto their tribal territories. Some Native American people resisted, notably the tribes of the Great Lakes region. Their resistance resulted in the Northwest Indian War (1785–95), which ended in victory for the United States.

Settlers chasing and killing Native Americans after an attack on a settlement in Ohio in 1791.

EFFECT ON THE ECONOMY

The war had a damaging effect on the new economy of the United States. Towns had been badly damaged and their populations had fallen. Merchant ships had been sunk or captured by the British, the tobacco trade with Britain (an important moneymaking export) slumped, and the price of goods in stores increased as inflation took hold. It would take time to rebuild the economy and fix the problems the war had created.

GLOSSARY

BAYONET
A long, pointed blade fixed to the end of a musket and used in close combat.

BOYCOTT
The act of refusing to use, buy, or have anything to do with something.

COLONY
An area of land in one country that people from another country settle in and control.

COLUMN
A military formation in which soldiers march in a long, narrow line.

COMMANDER IN CHIEF
The most senior leader of a military force.

CONSTITUTION
A set of rules that states how a country is to be organized and governed.

DESERTION
When a soldier leaves the armed forces without permission and has no plans to come back.

DIPLOMAT
An official who represents his or her country abroad.

DRILL
The process of training soldiers in military procedures, such as firing weapons, by making them perform the actions repeatedly.

EFFIGY
A model made to represent a person.

ENLIST
To join an army to fight in a war.

EVACUATE
To send people away from a place that has become too dangerous for them to stay in.

FIRECAKE
A very simple cake made with flour and water and cooked before an open fire. Made and eaten by the soldiers of the Continental Army.

INDEPENDENCE
When a country is on its own and is no longer controlled by another country.

HESSIAN
A soldier from the Hesse region of Germany who fought as a mercenary for the British army.

LOYALISTS
Americans who were on the side of Britain. Also known as Tories or King's Men.

MERCENARIES
Soldiers hired to fight for a foreign country. They were paid for their services.

MILITIA
A military force, especially one made up of civilians, not regular soldiers.

MINUTEMEN
American Patriots who pledged to be ready for battle at a minute's notice.

MORALE
The confidence and spirits of a person or group at a particular time.

MUSKET
A long-barreled gun that fired a ball of lead. It was fired from the shoulder.

NEUTRAL
When a country or a group of people stays out of a war and does not take sides.

PAMPHLET
A printed leaflet or booklet.

PARDON
To forgive someone for an error they have made, or an offense.

PARLEY
A meeting in which enemies discuss the argument between them. From the French word *parler*, meaning "to speak

PATRIOTS
People who love their country and support it. American Patriots fought against Britain. Also known as Rebels, Revolutionaries, Congress-Men, or American Whigs.

PEACE TREATY
An agreement made between the sides in a war to stop fighting.

PLANTATIONS
Large farming estates where crops were grown by workers, often slaves, who lived on the estate.

REBELLION
Resistance to authority, especially a government.

REDCOAT
Nickname for a soldier of the British army whose uniform included a red-colored topcoat. They were also called lobster backs."

REPEAL
The removal or reversal of a law.

RETREAT
When a defeated army leaves or withdraws from the battlefield.

REVOLUTION
When a government is replaced or overthrown and a new system is put in place.

SIEGE
A military operation in which an army surrounds a town or fortified place in order to capture it.

SKIRMISH
A fight or conflict involving a small number of people, and much too small to be a battle.

SLAVES
Human beings treated as property and made to work without pay by slave owners.

SMUGGLING
Bringing goods into or out of a country illegally, especially to avoid paying taxes.

TACTICS
A method of maneuvering troops in a combat situation.

TARRED AND FEATHERED
A punishment in which a person was covered with sticky tar onto which feathers were thrown.

TRUCE
An agreement to stop fighting for a time.

VOLUNTEER
Someone who willingly joins up to serve in an army.

WINTER QUARTERS
The resting place of an army during the winter season.

This edition published by Scholastic Inc.,
557 Broadway, New York,
NY 10012

Text, design, and illustrations © 2013
by Carlton Books Limited.
All rights reserved.

Published by Scholastic Inc.

SCHOLASTIC and associated logos are trademarks and/or registered trademarks of Scholastic Inc.

ISBN 978 0 545 57091 6

10 9 8 7 6 5 4 3 2 1

Printed in Dongguan, China

Senior Editor: Anna Bowles
Senior Art Editor: Andrew Watson
Design: Andy Jones
Illustration: Peter Liddiard
Picture Research: Gina McNeely
Production: Ena Matagic
Consultant: Dr. Matthew Kilburn

INDEX

PICTURE CREDITS

The publishers would like to thank the following sources for their kind permission to reproduce the pictures in this book.

KEY: NARA = National Archives and Records Administration, Washington; BAL = The Bridgeman Art Library;

LOC = Library of Congress, Prints and Photographs Division; MEPL Mary Evans Picture Library

p. 2 (Washington) BAL/Sterling & Francine Clark Art Institute, Williamstown, Massachusetts, USA, (Benjamin Franklin & William Howe) LOC, (Thomas Jefferson & Samuel Adams) NARA, (King George III) Thinkstock.com, (General Thomas Gage) Getty Images/ Hulton Archive, (John Burgoyne) Our Country, p. 2-3 (Battle of Lexington) Library of Congress, p. 4 (earth) Getty Images/Don Farr (map) www.davidrumsey.com, p. 5 (compass & King George III) Thinkstock.com, p. 6 (Native Americans) MEPL, (defending an attack) National Archives and Records Administration, Washington, (musket) Antique Military Rifles, p. 7 (barrels) Thinkstock.com, (stamp act) Library of Congress, (newspaper) Pennsylvania Journal, p.8 (Federal Hall & tar and feathering) LOC, (George Grenville) MEPL, (burning stamp act) NARA, p. 9 (Colden) Private Collection, (repeal) LOC, p .10 (ships at Boston harbour) American Antiquarian Society, Worcester, MASS. p. 10 (Crispus Attucks) Getty Images, p. 11 (Samuel Adams) NARA, (coffins) Getty Images, p. 12 (Lord North) MEPL, (hanging) Getty Images, (tea) iStockphoto.com, (East India Company) BAL/ Private Collection, p. 13 (Thomas Hutchinson) MEPL, (map) John Carter Brown Library, (swallowing bitter draught) NARA, (Boston Tea Party) LOC, p. 14 (Bostonians caged) LOC, p. 14-15 (Patrick Henry speaking) NARA, p. 15 (General Thomas Gage) Getty Images, (Patrick Henry) NARA, p. 16 (Paul Revere warning & Paul Revere) LOC, (map) Lexington Concord, p. 16-17 (Battle of Lexington) LOC, p. 17 (statue) David Pape, (pistol) iStockphoto.com, (retreat from Concord) NARA, p. 18 (Independence Hall & Benjamin Franklin) LOC, (Thomas Jefferson) NARA, (George Washington) BAL/Sterling & Francine Clark Art Institute, Williamstown, Massachusetts, USA, p. 19 (British warships) NARA, (Bunker Hill) National Army Museum, p. 20 (Continental currency) Our Country, (Thomas Paine) NARA, (Common Sense) LOC, p. 20-21 (Signing of Declaration) Architect of the U.S. Capitol, (Richard Henry) LOC, (Declaration of Independence) NARA, p. 22 (British officers) NARA, (Black loyalists) Topfoto.co.uk/ World History Archive, p. 22-23 (Surrender of Hessians) Anne S.K. Brown Military Collection, p. 23 (recruiting conscripts) Our Country, (Joseph Brant) LOC, (rifle) Photograph courtesy of Heritage auctions www.ha.com, p. 24 (Washington) LOC, (Minuteman) Our Country, p. 24-25 (Colonial Reenactors) Corbis/Richard T. Nowitz, p. 25 (Colonial types & Black soldiers) Anne S.K. Brown Military Collection, (Pitcher & firing drill) Corbis, p. 26 (British leave Boston) Anne S.K. Brown Military Collection, (Battle of Long Island) Our Country, (map) NARA, p. 27 (New York fire, Patriots in the Dumps & William Howe) LOC, (Forcing passage of Hudson) National Maritime Museum, Greenwich, London. All rights reserved. www.nmmimages.com, p. 28-29 (Washington crossing Delaware) Corbis, p. 29 (Mercenaries captured) Getty Images/MPI, (Battle of Princeton) LOC, (Battle of Trenton) BAL/ Chicago History Museum, USA, p. 30 (Battle of Germantown) BAL/ Chicago History Museum, USA, (map) Private Collection, p. 31 (John Burgoyne) Our Country, (General Horatio Gates & Rifleman) Anne S.K. Brown Military Collection, (Battle of Saratoga) Architect of the U.S. Capitol, (McCrea) LOC, p. 32 (Valley Forge) Our Country, p. 33 (Washington) BAL/Photo © Christie's Images/Private Collection, 33 (Washington & Lafayette) Library of Congress, (von Steuben) Anne S.K. Brown Military Collection, (von Steuben drilling troops) Our Country, p. 34 (Franklin) LOC, (French troops) Corbis, p. 34-35 (ships) NARA, p. 35 (Benjamin Franklin) BAL/Pennsylvania Academy of the Fine Arts, Philadelphia, USA, (John Paul Jones) U.S. Navy, (Naval battle) NARA, p. 36 (Sir Henry Clinton) BAL/American Museum, Bath, Avon, UK, (Battle of Monmouth) Molly Pitcher, (Washington) Our Country, p. 37 (Nathaniel Greene & Charleston) NARA, (Swamp Fox (Anne S.K. Brown Military Collection), p. 38 (Battle of Virginia Capes) U.S. Navy, (de Grasse) NARA, (map) LOC, (de Vimeur) The Bridgeman Art Library/Chateau de Versailles, France, Giraudon, p 39 (Battle of Yorktown & Lord Cornwallis) NARA, (Siege of Yorktown) BAL/Chateau de Versailles, France, Giraudon, (Capitol surrender) Architect of the U.S. Capitol, p. 40 (Blessings of Peace) Private Collection, (Unfinished painting) Winterthur Museum, p. 41 (map) LOC, (Treaty) NARA, (George Washington) BAL/© Collection of the New-York Historical Society, USA, p. 42 (James Madison) BAL/Musée Franco-Americaine, Blerancourt, Chauny, France, p. 42-43 (Signing of Constitution) Architect of the U.S. Capitol, p. 43 (Inauguration of President) BAL/Private Collection, (Constitution) NARA, p. 44 (slaves) NARA, p.44-45 (Washington at Mount Vernon) Superstock/The Art Archive, p. 45 (Attack on settlement) Corbis/Bettmann, (solider firing) Our Country

Every effort has been made to acknowledge correctly and contact the source and/or copyright holder of each picture and Carlton Books Limited apologises for any unintentional errors or omissions, which will be corrected in future editions of this book.